Saunter

Saunter

POEMS BY

Joshua McKinney

THE UNIVERSITY OF GEORGIA PRESS

ATHENS AND LONDON

Published by the University of Georgia Press
Athens, Georgia 30602
© 2002 by Joshua McKinney
All rights reserved
Set in ten on thirteen Aldus
Designed by Betty Palmer McDaniel
Printed and bound by McNaughton & Gunn
The paper in this book meets the guidelines for
permanence and durability of the Committee on
Production Guidelines for Book Longevity of the
Council on Library Resources.

Printed in the United States of America
06 05 04 03 02 P 5 4 3 2 1

Library of Congress Cataloging-in-Publication Data
McKinney, Joshua.
Saunter : poems / by Joshua McKinney.
p. cm.
ISBN 0-8203-2331-4 (pbk. : alk. paper)
I. Title.
PS3613.C56S28 2002
811'.6—dc21
2001045071

British Library Cataloging-in-Publication Data available

To My Friends

Contents

III. BATTEN

Acknowledgments

The author would like to thank the editors of the following publications in which many of these poems first appeared:

American Letters & Commentary: "Batten XXI, XXIII"
Bombay Gin: "Batten VI"
Colorado Review: "Batten XXXV"
CrossConnect: "Batten IV, XVI"
Denver Quarterly: "No Oasis," "Read," "Saunter," "Joinery," "Ends"
Faultline: "'Explosion in a Shingle Mill'"
First Intensity: "Batten I, II, III, XI, XIII, XV, XVII"
Gulf Coast: "Moment (without) Scars"
No Roses Review: "Unsound"
Pavement Saw: "Horizon," "Optique"
Quarterly West: "Batten XXV"
Salt Hill: "Batten VII, IX, X"
Sulphur River Literary Review: "The Problem & the Approach," "The Law"
Syllogism: "Batten V, XXII, XXIV, XXVIII, XXIX"
Volt: "An Opening," "Disfigured," "Truce," "Batten XXVII, XXX, XXXI, XXXIV"
Willow Springs: "Traces"
"The Elms" appeared in the chapbook *Permutations of the Gallery* (Pavement Saw Press 1996).
The fifteen poems in the title section of this book were published as a chapbook by Primitive Publications (1998).

I. *Saunter*

*I have met with but one or two persons in the course
of my life who understood the art of Walking, that is,
of taking walks,—who had a genius, so to speak, for
sauntering: which word is beautifully derived "from
idle people who roved about the country, in the
Middle Ages, and asked charity, under pretense of
going* à la Sainte Terre, *" to the Holy Land, till the
children exclaimed, "There goes a* Sainte-Terrer, *" a
Saunterer, a Holy-Lander. They who never go to the
Holy Land in their walks, as they pretend, are indeed
mere idlers and vagabonds; but they who do go there
are saunterers in the good sense, such as I mean.
Some, however, would derive the word from* sans
terre, *without land or a home, which, therefore, in the
good sense, will mean, having no particular home, but
equally at home everywhere. For this is the secret of
successful sauntering.*

—HENRY DAVID THOREAU

*We must take the feeling of being at home into exile.
We must be rooted in the absence of place.*

—SIMONE WEIL

Disfigured

Emptied owns escape.
Otherwise all
would be God. The
creatures look
through me in
the forest walking.
The only thing
piercing. Weather
I renounce and its

gratitude is mine.
The heron I
renounce and its
anguish is mine.
Millions awake. Twice
nude to begin with,
to pass into being
out of place,
hidden in the world.

An Opening

Subject to vertigo,
mountains swoon.
To break the cold,
a page whitens
its raw material
thicket ecstatically
still. Sheltered
in absence, geese
wedge their script

in thinnest air
a cello scales
some stairs. Risen,
a thought falls.
Yet an opening
remains, trembling,
in the same
continuous day
of the mountains.

Optique

Light scatters
the animals
magnetted to light
in the evening
dusk on a
road a stooping
man is a tree.
A thought flees
and so these

others. All whose
backs are scored
with the bleeding
zero of infancy
conforms to no
one. Out of many,
none. Near an end
the sum shook
free of its figures.

Joinery

... stone and flower
and blood as is
not a place, a thing at
all tokens of sound
are as a ladder
disguised. The trees
show their rings,
the animals, their veins.
In my backyard,

coordinates denied,
I saw a sound
move over the ground
bewildered. Swelling,
estranged, the back of
my hand was a letter
passed beyond proof,
a portion
of the beautiful.

Sap

First to arrive,
shadow whose voice
is registered
to every blow,
exposed. A child
is the lion.
Contrary, it goes
without saying.
A syntax of smoke.

Genius is conformity.
Small bright quick
in the grass
the wildflowers
in this grass
crying o reddest
green unhinged
o bluest blue.
Not needing to.

Askance

The rain is
smashed, its
modest revolt
weighs nothing
in aftermath
we rehearse serenity
its violence
held in
words worth

repeating. Do not
believe it.
The drama of
a familiar world was
never possible
penitence crushes
the mountain
in labor
does not aspire.

Means

The tongue's foul
genuflections
shatter in silence.
Where then?
If it turned out.
Or the sun's briars.
Aims a slant
reaching into.
My hand unborn.

I have not murdered
my angel wavering
like a thickcold
memory exhumed from
black lagoons down
in the basement,
down in the dark,
down in the ways
I want it to be.

Horizon

Still at a distance,
clouds in columns
measure other than
days. They appear
musically as one
avoids broken
glass, the odd-
numbered problems,
love's assignment.

A diamond will mean
water. Movement
of descent, outside
a center which is
outside a silence
forges the break
without echo
of which this
voice is issue.

M e r c y

Faster in reverse,
the wind across
this lake begins
a drowning. A new
grammar suffers
its inception
commands in questions.
Fish that flexes
in the hand

holds the delicate
body of prayer.
What can we do with it,
this fresher light
of shipwrecked eyes?
It is a reflection
where I have come,
silent at its edge,
to cast a stone.

Truce

Day after day,
what bond
will hold wherever
a birth is?
Scatters the gulls
and the small
sea stones
begin as one
thing, then

become the wind
attack the castle
in search of
a faith o tiny
hands, dirty
fingers! So
frightened now
that you are
needed.

Pilgrim

Dismemberment
does not destroy
absent in the act
the feet grate
radical against
the ground
a strange diagonal
predictable only in that
it has happened

to behave in new
positions, building
a city inside
that the gates
might close forever
on the traveler
who, imagining, stands
in a field, absent,
near total collapse.

Binge of Wane

Air is a field
where all is
harm planted a
bright bush,
a hesitation
between available
things. In black
wash recalled,
a sky, a sea

short of a dawn
spills likeness
by degrees.
o leprous
moon o
pearl
reversed . . .
bewilder
me.

Ends

Winter a hawk
huge in an oak,
its bare lightning
black, reversed
against the sky.
Lighter than
burning, the road
forecasted, un-
curves. As one

it will not beg.
No covenant save
proximity, vivid
in the distance
it is vicious,
it is spring—
a small force
erodes the moss
is on the stones.

New Library

But the same
fire. Was a moment
in each day we
could not find.
Stray through
the blinds, tree
shadows moved
over a page,
familiar and then

a fearful thing
that it might live
resorts to rage.
The stone against
the window was
a bird. Silent,
flame-slim, its
broken whole blazed
names unheard.

Saunter

The body's last
evidence, this
actual world
laughing too hard
to write it—at you
with your lunch
in your hair. No-
thing undeceives me
dreaming a man, I

am undeceived in
this actual world
bewildered hill to hill.
The air is the air.
Pain, too, is
the color of matter.
Obedient, I advanced
in attention
I moved no closer.

II. Traces

It is the dimension of absence that remains to be found.

—ROBERT SMITHSON

Traces

1

On the train you reread chapters
of the surrogate novel discarded
at the station. It had been raining all day,
and when you returned home
the sidewalk was scoured of the victim's outline.
Behind bolted doors, neighbors
squinted at the instances offered,
as through a peephole in a public restroom,
opening its intimate promise
on a similar compartment, its signatures
and calligrams scrawled and gouged
in the city's desperate margins. So it is
with the transient landscapes of the motel,
the inn, the motor lodge—
dear to us for their presence, absent
as it is, the gilt-framed Alps, the palms
surprising the peninsula at dawn—
they don't dare coincide. In some available scrutiny,
the least things wait for the imitation to end.

2

I knew a woman who had a man's name
written on her thigh. I read it there
and felt a sudden happiness, as if
the future had unglimpsed itself
in a rustle of maps unrolling. The sky
went slowly deaf, and on the radio
the popular song squared itself and vanished.

Later, driving home, I nearly died, hands
unfettered from the wheel,
a cicada chirping
in the car I was wondering from what place
I might speak and go unheard,
from what small scope, squeak. Instead of
music or ledgers, a kind of uninvented snow.
Or a burnished desert disguised as a garden.
Two serenities. Among our provisions, the finest
sadnesses, as if payment for our passage.
And then I thought of you,
at no distance, placing the small new-
voweled mouth behind bars, absurd tender.

3

On the bus you reread chapters
from the romance abandoned in the terminal.
The day's slack attention
festers as minutes and buildings smear
past—hammock vines strangling their host
trees. The pages lie in your hand, open
and unable to rise. Your eyes still
unbroken. Against the window
the horizon gets up, looms
over the tarred roof of the abattoir.
Afternoon is a nosebleed.
The fabulous domestic takes you
into its mouth. Somewhere someone is painting
a name beneath a bridge. Water is cool there.
In the black-and-white movie on a small screen
    in a trailer on the outskirts of town,
the moon rises red.

4

In a field I found a child's balloon
withered by its lostness, tether attached.
The tears of its parting were forgotten,
are forgotten, even as it wobbles
up over the heat of carnival lights
and the wheezy music, above the screams,
the spinning machines, dismantled,
loaded onto trucks at week's end
when the caravan leaves for a similar city.
Where we are going we are already old
and carnivals close the streets.
The abeyance between notes is filled
with the smell of tires burning.
The reliquary stuffed with photos was
forgotten in the portable toilet. Nostalgia
left yesterday with its accordion.
Hurry. The tourist bus is departing for the temple.
We cannot think of dying. We stand
at the base of tall strangers. We move
and out of this we come to the world again—
no picture to replace it.

The Elms

The trees receive their shadows.
In such an image, the bark, the body,
just because it wears a shower, accumulates,
distilled into a girl in a soldier suit,
a man sprouting arrows. Elsewhere, notes
thicken in a staff and liberating columns
waver under the pressure of distance. I
am walking here between symmetrical walls
of memory where the sidewalk cracks
under my toes. I wear this silly armor.
If such catastrophe occurred, what name
could tell me anything more? A brief and
morning breeze early overhead flashes
as again in autumn a taste for it
rises up out of ghost leaves to hang
above the painted house. It is not mine.
Nor the absent shadows which cross
the lawn, well-groomed to the birdbath
evincing the sun. No need to look up.
Air: the corporeal part of trends.
Look over there, avert. The anonymous
face of the young victim twists, martyred
by naming. Compressed into pictures,
he enters the little house at the end
of the lane. I was walking between
the cities of honest men where trees
had crossed whole words without hindrance.
I were walking plural when the armies
passed, leaving the musical city.
The disease of absence captures
the imagination. Incarnate, incarnate.

Marvelous are the distances of the road,
tall faces written on the billboard's
anatomy, gaunt armor, its surface
scored over and over. Looking back,
the pillars recede with their ribbons.
Beneath the shade trees where the light is
brightest, the last leaves chatter into flame.

Unsound

The ocean is small and dreams
of the recent past, wound that was
beginning. From the pulp of the vocable,
all space and movement, the word
kicks. Where conjugates silence,
the scream is driven—*form*,
a darkening rose, two-headed,
the perfectionist's nightmare.

If I conceive these instruments
without taking leave of the future,
I erase its pain. The screen is
black at first, then white.
At variance with reason,
the skull's cross section rises
from the grainy borders of the womb.
Already legible, the heart, the tiny cage.

Already the naming has begun.

No Oasis

Where God is absent, creation can begin.
Now, before the silence of what's next,
the author disappears and starts again.

At any point upon the track, a thin
light leaks through cracks left in a text.
Where God is absent, creation can begin

to blend and clash. The spirit is to win
as air defeats *the* air: without context,
the author disappears and starts again

to make a world, a golden wheel to spin
it on—and all its method circumspect.
Where God is absent, creation can begin;

it leaps into a distance without end,
where land moves always. As the wind directs,
the author disappears and starts again

to ask a question of the shadow in
each word: an echo in the clamor of a next
where God is absent. Creation can begin
to disappear. The author starts again.

The Law

Flatness knows the immediacy of shape:
eyes in the dark geometric movement,
teeth and claws blooming
beneath the tongue's tendrils.

We empty the Bag of Names
before us, its pitiful pile
exhausted with choices.

Throw *river* into a river and it floats away.

All day the ordinary occurs
without witness. We sleep
in the glow of such freedom, thought
previously miraculous. Catastrophe has driven
the dream of two-legged Happiness out
into the jungle without applause.

The Problem
& the Approach

The untimely death of verbs
obstructs a stream of experiments.

We come out of a café to find
it has stopped snowing. This is
mastery of higher order infusing the
gutters and shop windows.
The world is for sale
here, simple and deep,
a four-letter tree the child climbs
en route to the aegis of constellations.

We come out of a café to find
a familiar white blanket, the street
somehow as we had left it
behind with the labor of trees.

The point of view is mediational,
reflected in the beautiful
shop windows where the trees and
street lamps are drawn in
and we are free to think
of the cold as a thing melting.

Moment (without) Scars

—baited,
anterior to crisis,
the phantom rigorously
derived from memory.
Like the man who lost
his thumb in
a threshing machine—
borders of a new continent
on his sleeve.
Such instants cramp
under thought's inflection
stopping to stare into
space, a hyphen
still dogging the date of
its birth. Blossoms
infect the surface
and we return
to the man without a thumb,
the way he palms his wife's
breast, how his pen
spells disaster
in a sinister track
leading into wilderness
where the map's **X**
stands for everything,
and the jar, exhumed, is empty.
The rest is waiting.

Lake Effect

never the same waves.

It agrees, but
how? Whatever burns down

Like a candle the eye alludes
to many abysses

The sight of rows   breaks
you   the beautiful

emergency I did not dream
        some of the drawings like agony

                        and this
hand-me-down sweater with its missed
stitch
        opens
                to the wind

"Explosion in a Shingle Mill"

Critic's description of Marcel Duchamp's
Nude Descending a Staircase, Armory Show, 1913

Despair faults every beautiful monster.
Thick with idleness, innocent
of its own corruption,
the thin air of grief gathers its paper
flowers and descends.
There is nothing to love.
The bright rain leaves the street.
Once there was another state.
At this point it needed I seemed only
to go on breathing to escape influence.
In error, yes. The lateness of these
days pesters some impossible paradise.
Disempowered by new snow, the young
enter parks, edge under the dark
halo of monuments where they try
to save themselves with language.
A terrible rigor rules this fiction.
Its outcomes span the instant
as a festoon of paper figures. Joining
hands, any pair can stop painting, turn
from the iron face of the pioneer,
and pause, kissing in the cold.
It ends there. The walk back to car
or apartment is rote as old snow
scored by footprints' binary dirge.
In its fullest development,
the wind remains unaccomplished—

virtue as penance, painfully tranquil,
recollected. Before she became
an architect, the child could raze
the dead icon, the mundane object.
Green is as green does: little oceans
with right angles or an arctic
zone where someone scatters a house.
The bright rain leaves the street,
paralyzed at the surface, the caffeine
of recalcitrant stone. There is nothing
to love. A day will come when cackles rise
from cereal boxes and the old return
to leavening, incongruous parks.
We cannot spend that day
in explanation. Our acts our angels are.

Read

Waiting
for the end
of the
indeterminate
now where
context becomes
clear. As if
to peel the day from the desk calendar
prematurely were a kind of curse—
worms in a can; fish in a kettle.

"Here I was perplexed," wrote Frederick Douglass.
"I found it was 'the act of abolishing,'
but I did not know what was to be abolished."

Perplexed, a child picks the scab from a wound
where years later he will finger a scar,
the body's Braille committed
to the memory of what
it meant in the absence of
service   the word alone
imperative perhaps
or adrift
without cargo
a silence
inconsolable.

III. Batten

I left the well-house eager to learn. Everything
had a name and each name gave birth to a new
thought. As we returned to the house every object
which I touched seemed to quiver with life. That
was because I saw everything with a strange, new
sight that had come to me. On entering the door I
remembered the doll I had broken. I felt my way
to the hearth and picked up the pieces. I tried
vainly to put them together. Then my eyes filled
with tears; for I realized what I had done, and for
the first time I felt repentance and sorrow.

—HELEN KELLER,
"Everything Had a Name"

I

Wafer-thin, the morning's   green amnesia breaks
Against waking   more oblivious than sleep
A brief sense of   being lost   then
Night resumes. There is   a space that takes
To living—so beautiful   you can weep
Your eyes blue   find fragments shored tight
Against a vaulted sky   the slightest crack
And it comes down   o intricate heap
Of language now   waked   lazy   alert
Affright I fell through   the word-
Wood pressed back   dark white

II

This being one, stranger   at bent-arm's length
Or "The last of   the cowboys"   a formation
Bones in a field   inside the body shattered
At large. Cruel artifice   takes strength
Less than hours   the faces of succession
Love forgot the other side   of the coin mattered
Less than ours, we thought   no   more
Should a vital vocal   wind still move
Its stop-place charge   not seen but heard—
A fire in long grass   behind
A green door   open

III

Strange diagonal
That smacks the frame
And still, what ought
And break upon the will
Desire's full. The figure
A name; the noiseless
Untamed, turns in space
A mark appears
As when a boot-toe
Kicks up, unsought
Gleams! At quick core
Small shutter
And then

of thought
   against the glass
to buck
   is dark
in the fog lacks
   vowel caught
and then
   before the foot   a grace
in the dirt
   a carapace
a heart-
   bangs back now
I start

I V

The difference between   the river road
Its dark traveling   under the sheen of
Hard thought, and say   a kid riding
The sofa, shrieking   "Mr. Toad! Mr. Toad!"
Is accident   the comparison   above which
Gulls have now begun   to squawk or sing
Clashes with the idea   that this is not
A poem. Pick one: a dead whale or a stove boat
On the beach   sudden flotsam
Flings speech back at   itself   by chance
A knot   a thing

V

And it came to pass   that color and pain
The maps that name   (cross out) the waves of us
Disclose an image   traced in dust   small scope
Some "must have meant"   muddied by tall rain
And then we stare   another morning just
For fun, free of plot, and   then—envelope
Paper, pen—notion   polished into fact
And it comes to pass   that the sheen of place
Melts in the palm as one   by one we grope
Toward two. Not here,   unless fear is
A form of   hope

VI

An attic full of frames   and thinnest voice
Blames glare on green   outside   the sun springs up
Lean and bare, a gun   and all about the town
Quick colors cut a groove   through gutters moist
With dew. Awash in   this high room   a cup of
Ink reflects the splash   enormous sound
Without a single source   drink now   but don't forget
To drown. Off course   the spray-smash slaps
All empty space   the strewn-about
Is bound to slaves of   place   which risen
Slip, and won't   bow down

VII

Bright beasts in the field know
The ground under their feet is clean
In all the earth tiny angels   little
Lower than Death the last
Through slow showers of fire   go
Unnumbered, the strange beasts stride
Their blonde legs shiny as grass
Burned bright as sky new-crowned   cast
Upon our heads and hands what dominion
Gives is taken back in blacks and reds
Any color kindled but a little   is wrath
What claws of light to tear
Tight union you have!

VIII

And I kept not my mouth   with a bridle
And the world fled   before me out of sight
And unto me it came   again transformed
And I established not   my path   idle
I went and the way   was dark with light
That bent above the days   as words new-shorn
Will heap up as sound   crash down   and free
All those who are   as strangers bound outright heed
Danger signs. To point   away   to mourn
Is vain. A thing   that has the will
To be is   born

I X

The eye can cloak
Rage for fact. The smoke
Of meat. The slow beasts
The past its noise. The will
To pace, a place still
Moon can part the
Blot out the names of
Word of my flesh
The days fall now!
The shall, the have
Cast down the thrones

can act in the next-noon
twists up in praise
graze   they bawl and give
is but a room
slack with cease   what phase of
blood?   what joy can save
art?   sword in my bones
that melts to spell
come cut the was
of me   beat back the dead
and live

X

The eye that burns   this light   happy to meet
Itself again and turn   back dark   is shield
From shall to have   from field to field   the past
Withholds no good thing done   upon the street
Such tales are told   what mercy sped   revealed
Itself and spoke?   what palm bled gold but cast
Out green? O round about!   o compassed heart
Of sound nouned up   with ends   a means is veiled
In space a silence speaks   a stop-gap vast
As things unnamed   break form
Leap to start   next last

XI

Oh silent noise   of joyful flood
Refresh the roar, fire-   clap the blood
Come, spell a word   quick as air
Fur thick on a fish   scale bright under wing—
All borders mesh   and hum as a taut string
Struck. They say a shell   hurls back the sea
Against a void   a wish   a plea
To make experience   bless not lest you be
Blessed the same   in name   what shall we do?
Doubtful sound   new-blurred   extinguish
Mind that thought   may drown   uncoil
In a hot spring   flash

XII

The is a place and a   much in and done
End as in race. End in   at in vast trace
Skipped like rams at   vends slam oppose
Not an inch in there   to hear   lends long gone
And gone where I will   I will them   unspaced
The sea saw and fled   red the one three rose
In of an won. At to put   to put show
Suffer the caught   not a can   can a face
Close in look look or   book then not close?
Can shook run in   at?   how one can
In now   suppose

XIII

More than the stealing out   the stealing in
More than they that watch   for loving
Then were our mouths filled   with moving laughter
And strange birds trilled   out of dark morning
When origins shout,   must approval range   sing
As though some tall wall   gleamed?   lofty rafters
Draped with rope. Barns and stalls, hopes hung as tack
In sparkling dust where children   swung as kings
The broken glass   behind a wall   faster than
Wings, refracts   the light
Small eyes look back   after

XIV

I will lift up my hands   in the same name
The right, the left   the bands of vein and blood
And tear what warp or weft   still cleaves my tongue
To shame. I will be   next in the next   a flame
Sharp as leaves of speech   the face in the hood
Shall not be mine; the   line that grieves for
young days lost will loop   and find that it is gone
That where truth   stood once   there is a flood
Of noise. White, stray past   this place   that sprung
Now has no guilt, no   grace   no
Edge but one   a song

XV

Expelled, a name   begins a violent practice
A parody, a same   new nothing   I
Am fearful and wonder   fully unmade   you
Too, are a flight, a shade   of once or bliss
That sought escape   from things   and so we try
To write an is. One note   softens into
All. Arpeggios harden   into walls
The beasts stay   put as in a zoo   a lie
Of long and long   what might be true
Is true for them   outside the
Dull throng   starts
When calls pass   through

XVI

Compassed by was   the lion's mouth is kind
A voice, unstill, and   then high up the heart
Of it. The wind is shrill   the wound beset
By sutures. Healed   the sound of futures winds
Into a tomb tight-sealed   but torn apart
The edge is read, and red   as real can get—
It will not end. One bone   in a field   one
Shard in the hand   expands to lend a start-
Ing place. It glides!   it skates   the body   text
Of slate that broke   makes pain
A note that gone   begets

XVII

Said to excel, the shapes   of grief subject
Themselves to rule   their dear commands cast
Out and cull. The fear that makes the many thrive
Can make the world   handsome cities reflect
This fact. What will not last gets talked about
Until it turns to stone   no tool can scribe
An arc of smoke, crazy   its weight less than
Air. The children watch it   twist and shout
That it spells fire   they say it looks alive—
Some sign of   a heaven
Where no thing   can survive

XVIII

The window gives back   nothing   imprisoned
The eye screws   into sharper focus   hacks
Through sense to   expectation   ideas paid out
Become a thin blue   thread the legend
Marks as river. Read right the map attacks
The site. Agent of matter   what light laid
Low-rent terrain   to glass   what spelled
Can break the fictive   voice   where grass springs
Back, the tracks are gone the droves and wheels
Of choice parade   the malady of wanting
To make   unmade

XIX

Returned to speech after which nothing else
Need be said. Enactment the staining means
Of thought, meanders over place and back
I had the closing unison of bells
In mind. I had in mind the posing of lean
Faces, hungry, kind in this way the lack
Of silent spaces cannot stray   it fits
As mirrors lie: in tune but absence keens
Inside each word a cry reversed
Can crack a tongue in two   lose half
Reopen its attack

Attention spans   the smallest gap   revealed
Time ran out   into the day   a trap
For false returns. Cheated   the moon is one
It lugs the sea ashore   and more concealed
Than sand, a snug thought   marks a map
As land. Precise mirages   carved in stone
Defrost, vanish in   ruins reversed   and speech
Its outer dark rehearsing loss   is sold as scrap
To mend. At every phase   the moon is done
For all we know   beneath the waves
The beach is   gone

XXI

Struck down by remorse   the air refuses
To appear. A stiff sun   sweeps   the field
Loose, and tiny   creatures   in the grass
Retreat. Panicked, manic   whatever use is
It taunts us to listen   what small life ' yields
A song lit with want? What   haunts the past
Must haunt the next   with the furious   dross
Of memory. By choice   the quick child kneels
To find the flash—the shard of wicked glass
That calms him, so dawn   already flush with loss
Can   pass

XXII

All that is solid   melts into air
A warfare accomplished   so that the straight
May bend, the late   fend for itself
And the day conspire   with sight to tear
Pages from picture   books   for who can wait
For a thing to end? If one   should   doubting   delve
Beyond the walls   and find them gone   then what?
Shouting could not   echo back   and the gates
Would swing open   onto doubt   could a self
Crack a word in half   and the sound of that
Be   wealth?

XXIII

for Phelan

Your hands, twin	spiders scamper from the plate
Where landscapes slide	together on a fault
Your mind pries	open to release the dove
Below the tiny house	you must create
The cat's rush, uncoiled	from a bush you exalt
The beetle and the worm—all	lives that move
Beneath the surface	still your will to rage
Is blurred, so that	the words you make are caught
By surprise, shaken	loose from the need to prove
Such things as age	the whiteness of
A page	or love

XXIV

Out of insistence   a flurry of means
Into the hurried dark   storm whams   taken
Away. I am a person   like simple words
Even in the stream   distinguished   it seems
New radiance will fall   full from a shaken tree
It is a time to loot and   hew   the birds
Gather like soot on   the backs of the beasts
What matters least is   that they awaken
What remains to be   dreamed   will be incurred
By and by as the static   once increased
Is   heard

XXV

An unpronounceable name went and came
Over stones at evening   when the various
Things had set, gone into shadow returned
Tall it came, one   and the other the same
So it was quiet in the house and there was
Asking and asking. Even   night   learned
To wait. No word had come to end the phrase
And tongues stumbled   dumbly over teeth
Something to say something precarious
As empty space, was   meant in the end   it turned
Out to be nothing this language of earth
That   burned

XXVI

Spring! The trees fly up   to their birds   the breeze
Heavy with flowers   hurts us like a grave
That, despairing of   its void   slams shut
What stay against   the gathering ease
When the senses cloy   and topple like a wave?
And does that not cause   everything to halt?
Sight is an oath   where the eye marks a pause
In light. The mouth holds   a mirror   is slave
To intimate breath   death is clearer   but what
Do we insist on   then? when did this cause
All   that?

XXVII

The love in question comes   to light in the last
A lamp, a matter of hands   of sums   the shadow
It throws is fatter than   before and where
It lands, it grows, a pause   in the pledge   vast
As a different   direction   how many know
Silence only as   objection? aware
Sober, syllables   stand waiting   her
Will come to us and where   them will go
Is a surprise   am I still anywhere
Near the question?   allow me
To answer   from there

XXVIII

Continues in a border region   where
Light filters through   some thin reality
A refuge for a fantasy dispelled
Held in abeyance   huge with stillness   there
On the shelf from whence it fell and   shattered   re-
Invented as a thing   that cannot be held
Can you kindly smile content with the ex-
Ample? Could you blindly   kindle a city
Of silhouettes? And would you   ring
A bell to call all to see   who gets to sing
Next? do tell

XXIX

A violent luck spread   upon the low
And sere—a lost book   brought precisely here
To be read as words   or bust   or must we bring it
Wholly undone? Some   thought it a show
Of force, or worse   a rugged tool to tear
The place, though   never completely working
Others stayed outside   the trace forever
Shall we begin, then   to hide it somewhere
Between *in* and *on*   someplace near a thing
We cannot mention?   and never weep
Never   sing

X X X

The distance on the look   touches each fact
Therefore one does not   such seeing took
A torch will parch the core   now summer's tent
Hangs over us and stirs   the vapid act
Unspent. At sunrise   the horizon shook
Smoke from a neighboring state   o ghostly scent
The gangs along the road   are gone
Their bright clothes   erased   the sign I mistook
For a man reads, "The days are   few   repent"
Nailed to a tree   braced against
A new zone   event

XXXI

So when I came here   descended through clouds
Winded, shorn of name   entire   the fire turned
To look at me. Agreement   not to tell
Later, spell-broken   houses lost   the road
A safety zone, a scar   once cut   what was learned
Was token to none save those   who knew well
But had forgotten. Ash   gave nerve   hot-wired
A will to good. If blood   could   it would burn
Flesh to a word no urn   could hold   none to spell
The tired. Save   for the wild
I would have   fired it all

XXXII

A landscape like this   will not support a scar
Partial to its latest effort   the eye
Closes against itself   and then I saw
That form was draped   upon the word   and there
Upon the brilliant shape   where colors die
Upon the page. The first   task was to flaw
With names the things that   never asked for
Voice. The choice it brings   to speak   or to cry
Out in formless grief   when tooth and claw
Read in the past   tense   become relief
A truth   or law

XXXIII

A rare or casual vagrant   flits across
A barren line   during migration   its
Stiff sentence outsmarts   the tender
Climate, which calmly rends the   air to toss
Tin from a barn roof   far into this
Field. It is proof   enough to render
All else false. And this   what will not yield
Becomes a living thing   passes on   fits
Into the hot silence   the eye that mends   here
Now, while the structure   stands open
Healed   what splendor

XXXIV

It was good to hear   from you   and I
Thought of that time   near the wood when we
Saw the bright flash of a   bird part the green
Wall of that world. It burned   the sight   yes? our eyes
Closed as it flew straight at us   we were three
Live things then. And when we looked   once more   keen
To see where it had gone, one   of us never
Should have tried to guess   its name   suddenly
It was a word, much less than   it had been
Your mouth was   the cruelest hue I had ever
seen

XXXV

A carelessness   sufficient to the day
Ransacks the trees   sound comes of no source
Forces the bloody cracks   in the eye   grown fat
With sight, to tremble   out of air   flayed
Down to acrobatic glee   a swallow's course
In flight is vatic   free   where it is
At any point cannot be   made to break
Off course, there was no call for remorse
For falling up. I forgot   the way back
And yet I felt remorse   what do you make
                           of that?

Notes

The quoted portion of "Read" was taken from *Narrative of the Life of Frederick Douglass, an American Slave, Written by Himself.*

In "'Explosion in a Shingle Mill,'" the line "Despair faults every beautiful monster" was taken from Robert Smithson's essay "What Really Ruins Michelangelo's Sculpture."

"Our acts our angels are," a portion of the final line of "'Explosion in a Shingle Mill,'" was taken from the Epilogue to Beaumont and Fletcher's "Honest Man's Fortune," which is the epigraph to Emerson's essay "Self-Reliance."

In "Batten XXII" the line "All that is solid melts into air" was taken from *The Communist Manifesto.*